THE SOULS OF FREE FOLK

*Kara—
enjoy this book! I look forward to more conversations + recommendations while working together.
—Hayden*

THE SOULS OF FREE FOLK

Josiah Golson

CHATTANOOGA   Polyphemus Press   2018

Text and artwork copyright © 2018 by Josiah Golson.

All rights reserved. No part of this publication may be reproduced, distributed, or transmitted in any form or by any means, including photocopying, recording, or other electronic or mechanical methods, without the prior written permission of the publisher.

Polyphemus Press
900 Vine Street Suite 2
Chattanooga TN 37403

polyphemuspress.com

Printed in the United States of America

Library of Congress Control Number: 2018931598
Randy Josiah Golson, Jr.
The Souls of Free Folk/ Josiah Golson.
128 p. 17.78 x 25.4 cm.
ISBN-13: 978-0-9997747-1-7

First edition.

Photograph p. 121 courtesy of Jaya Todai.
Text set in Charis SIL.

Dedicated to my Family:

Randy Sr., Pamela,
Christina and Caleb

ONE

In my cloud of sweet slumber and youthful dreams
I envisioned my perfect life
Complete with a destiny of my design
And nature yielding to my desires…

But I Woke to a Pain that I could not comprehend
Pain that would not reconcile with Reason
Pain that defied my Dreams
As it warped my Personhood into a Problem

Nothing in my cabinet could cure or contain this Ache
that reduced my skin to a shadow
And I, broken in two,
Voiced fragmented cries for wholeness

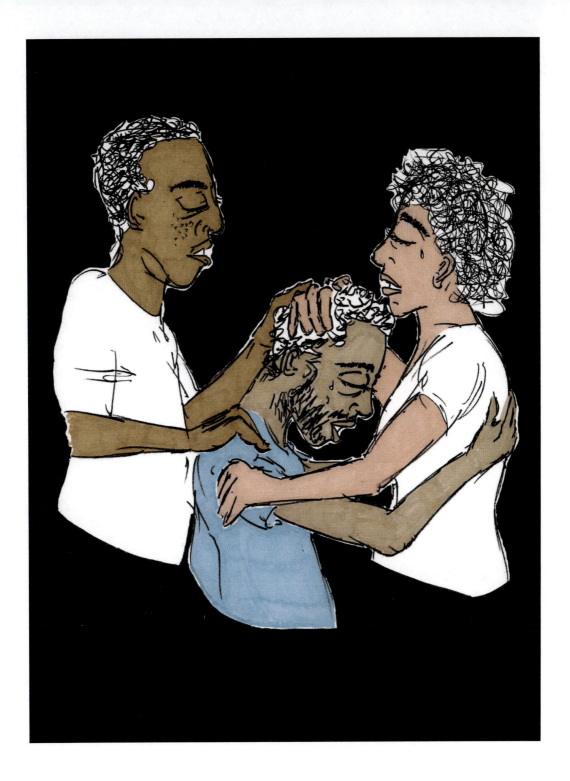

Mother held me in her arms, prayers and tears
as Father searched for scripture to sustain my slipping spirit
And in the sculpture of their embrace, I sought Sanctuary
Sanctuary that I had long taken for granted

I felt Mother feel my pain as her own
in supreme and tragic feminine empathy
And I saw her ache to receive me back in
If it meant I could kick and dance once again

I saw Father recognize dark memories
reflected in the tears falling from my eyes
And as he wiped away his own
He continued his eloquent prayers, like Psalms to the Throne

With my eyes dry from weeping
And my voice soar from wailing
and the Pain not yielding
I crawled from my bed

Weary, and feeling that my life was found wanting

Wondering if Winter was laying its claim

and fearful for the night that awakened the dormant demons from the depths of my being,

I force myself outside to seek a cure…

I step onto the barren streets of suffering
and taking in the scene,
I feel my feet fade from beneath me

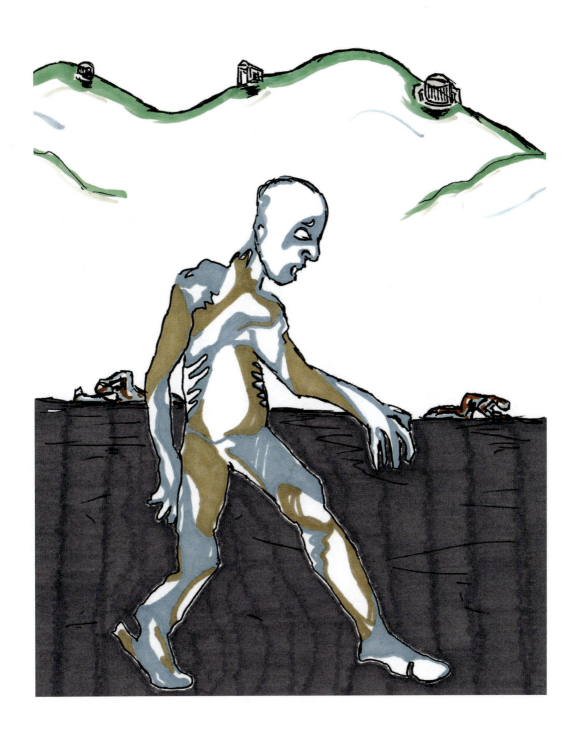

Our City is not set Upon a Hill
But in a Valley of Dreams Deferred

I trek through this Valley in the shadow of wealth

There is no self-care
For there's no knowledge of Self

My search for medicine takes me outside of myself
through battlefields covered in antebellum ashes…

And among bodies on the brink of a beautiful bang,
before falling like shells of lost potential

I hear the confusing cries of a would-be prophet,
Who has in him a dozen novels but can't write his own
Name

I hear the screams of a woman,
Ravaged by the hands of horrid and habitual
Inhumanity

I see the brutal blows to my brothers and sisters,
Who are invisible to Lady Justice,
Oblivious from behind Her blindfold

They are bound to a chain gang linked by history,
Pacing down a "more perfect" path to ruin

They are lost in the legalese of a courtroom
Where "colorblindness" is a defect, not a virtue

Laws are informed by the apathy and lucre of the few,
Ruling over the bodies and minds of the many

Our stories are reduced to stereotypes

While we watch the watchmen with our trust issues

Carrying these horrors in place of my hopes,
I get to the doctor, who knows I'm Broken
but cannot assemble me
And sees me as a number, not a Face

In the window of the clinic walls,
I rage at my Reflection
Why don't my genes match my dreams?
Why my curious complexion?

Back outside I join the hustle, or "pursuit," with The People

As we search for our places like mimes for their voices

For so long, we've waged a losing war with borrowed words of privilege

While others in the "pursuit" trade their American Dream for American Green

We seek cinematic love in the darkness of the club
But romance eludes us like the sweetness of whiskey and white

And in this loneliness, we linger and long for the light

Saturday night gives way to Sunday morning
And bodies pour out of club parking lots
Into church pews
We beg forgiveness for sinning
for thinking
for being

But our prayers are answered by the continuing lashes of life
As we suffer crucifixion, with no sign of Christianity

Amidst the rising Cityscape

We seek our shrinking spots in the proceeding plans

And our elders left behind beg for crumbs from the table built in their backyard

But even I remember as I stumble about

No one cared about this garden until roses forced their way through the concrete

Now those roses are pulled and sold as the concrete gives way to cash

We spend our days seeking solitary solace in a common song
that we never sing together

Until restlessness gives way to rage and some try to right the wrongs with hopeless riot

Mothers and Fathers, Friends and Neighbors, Fragmented Nations
All mourn lives lost,
Quickly and slowly,
To the fate of our Bodies
Bodies deemed cages rather than creations

And we tread from grave to grave
Veiled from the freedom we have yet to feel

All night, I am now haunted by the faces of My People
Searching for themselves
My pain merely echoes the agony we've carried all this time
Like breathing contradictions at the mercy of the clock

So under a dim, yellow Light,
Bracing my weary body and waning mind
In the clear moments between my anguish and agony
And fed up with the fear of tomorrow's tyranny
I search for the spark of My Soul

TWO

Pushing through the smog of this ailing society
I seek my Spirit beneath the contemporary, in the secrets of history

And I seek to illuminate the lives of those who I didn't see before my illness

Who are we?

Where is our Home?

Should we abandon this road we've travailed?

Or see what the end is going to be?

Is this suffering putting all I know to sleep...

Or waking an unknown life I have yet to claim?

I muse on the markings of my Mother
and sift the sadness that steals her shine

I whisper the words of my Father
and wonder why his poetic rhythm is rebuffed by life's routine

Taking the language and love of My Folks as my only true treatment,
I tread through the known and unknown temples of my town,
with my eyes open for the faintest flickers of freedom

For maybe it's in these flames where the Truth resides
Where Our healing hides

Back on the street

There is Struggle

But there is still Movement

I build the strength of my steps by following the determined path of those who Marched before me

Even where there is no Movement
Stillness and Silence speak infinite Strength
I awe at how we sit and stand in immortal resistance

In this constant fight,
Healing seems a luxury we cannot afford…

Yet I witness wounds resolve through radiant acts of Love

Realizing the supernatural power of Love,
I use it as my lens, to excavate the Beauty that is buried like treasure
beneath the sand of our aching skin

Love reveals the Shine of my Sisters in their confident and courageous stances

With open ears,
I now decipher the Prophet's cries into honest Oral Tradition,
as he tries to piece together Past, Present and Promise

I see the wounded woman soothe her skin
to reclaim it from the hands that forced her screams

I receive the sweet salvation from stories of Song,
Harvested in records like revolving spirits,
Waiting to be released

The spirits reveal themselves,
like the regal woman on the plantation's wilderness of white
She was a Queen
Even when cotton was "king"

I enter the Museum,
And receive antidotes
As I awaken with others to the glory of our unclaimed Wealth

We recognize and revere our Kings and Queens
Who created their own crowns

Emerging from the Museum, I caress the graffiti on our City walls
Translating them into their hieroglyphic essence

The lines return my touch with an embrace that empowers me with
History and Inheritance
Heroism and Happiness
Healing and Hope

Filled with regeneration and revelation,
I now see my body, our Bodies
in beautiful hues of Truth

All this time
We were Technicolor children
trying to fit into a static "black and white" world

And You, born of a thousand bloodlines and stories,

Must realize that you can no longer carry them in silence

Are You brave enough to embrace them and affirm Your worth to the world?

Are You Brave Enough
To Love the Real You?

Our own fight for Freedom is embedded in the very fabric of the flag:

The Red passion of our spilt blood

The White light of our uncompromising truths
And the beautiful music of our Blues

We move through the darkness like lamps of Love
Lamps that illuminate our eternal essence amidst the abyss

We are heirs to a Glory that will never give out

No longer do we sing hand-me-down hallelujahs
Nor do we bear the chastisement made by a conspiracy of chains

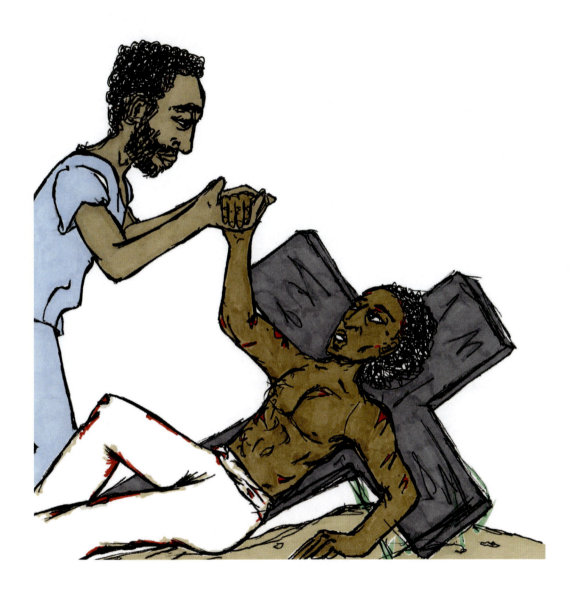

For We Love our way through the lashes of life

And this bold, brilliant and beautiful Love breaks the Pain and reveals the Balm of our Souls

Our Souls, that grew beneath the earth like seeds of freedom

To spring forth and produce the fruitful sounds that feed the world in every season

I now feel the medicine in my melanin
I see the miracle amidst the madness
I hear the music in my movement

And I behold Us,
and recognize that our Cure is as plain as the beauty on our Faces
The beauty I find in Me
The beauty I find in We

We, who flew as sacred fire out of the scattered ashes of our painful past

We, who claim the present infinitely more than those bound by their ill-gotten bounty

We, who improvise the future with the beat of our celestial drum

I bring forth my spark in a rush of release

The Spirit is willing, and the Flesh must break Free

THREE

I emerge from the smoke of sorrow
Following my spark and the love flowing to my limbs

And my feet, once chained down in historic hurt, now float in a dance of freedom

Wide-awake with awe-inspired eyes, I see the endless possibilities of my life

For I see the potential of My People

We are vibrant vessels of greatness,
with royalty in our rhythm
and Wealth in our walk

Mother, do not mourn the dark morning
For your singing and smile are what bring the bright Dawn

Father, do not forsake your muse
For your "unanswered" prayers may be your greatest Poetry

I surrender to Color

I surrender to Sound

I speak life into every part of my Being

My praise does not depend on the ears of others
Nor does my color require the eyes of the crowd
But through self-affirmation, I attract my own Tribe

From stumble to stride, our Movement on the street manifests itself into a parade of Pride and Power

We rebuild our broken bodies through brazen steps of whim

And in turn, we become the Green of this Valley and this City's Beautiful Gate

We sweat out the smell of guilt
To wear the scent of Grace

The Glow works its way up
From the feet to the face

Our instruments feed the friction for the flame of our healing

As our hurt burns away, our Bodies shine brighter than the brands we've chased for so long

Now we all heed the Prophet
As his cries soften to clear and confident speech
of our Purpose and place in the puzzle

We behold the grace of the Woman

Who, in wholeness, sings the strength of her survival and moves the limbs of her liberty

With such music, we defeat the famine and reap the "Harvest Wonderful"

And we shine as the cultivated Vibes mend our bones with beauty

We found our Faith in the Spirit of our Sound
And not in a religion, revised to keep us bound

I emerge from the water with a new sense of peace
Baptized by Ancestors who were once lost at sea

Our Gospel is the Glory and Greatness of this Land

Democracy survives and thrives on The Jazz

We change the narrative pushed on us
And create our own Classic
No matter who writes or signs the laws
They can't legislate our Magic

Riot yields to Renaissance,
   as We reshape the power structure
The Wealth is in our hands
   for We have the Culture

And finding the Light within
I sing with new thoughts, flesh and clothes

To a chorus that sounds of Ten Million Freed Souls…

Outside of my cloud of dreams
I build a destiny with My People doing the same

We rise and sing together for our children,
Walking the world naked and not ashamed.

THE LINER NOTES

Dear Gentle Reader,

The Souls of Free Folk is but a flower that I hope to contribute to the garden of incredible art, literature, music, and genius inspired by the African American experience. It has been a privilege to write and illustrate words and images that are rooted in the brilliance and resolve of my parents, ancestors, community, and a culture that time and time again has transformed the world.

As Black culture has forged its path out of bondage and on a continuing journey to freedom, I believe it to be essential that I share a few of the many inspirations behind this work. It's my hope so that in your journey with my story, you will also explore or re-explore these timeless works that can provide insight, healing, and guidance for us all.

With Love and Light,

Josiah

Literature & Poetry

Frederick Douglas, *My Bondage and My Freedom* (1855)

W.E.B. DuBois, *The Souls of Black Folk* (1903)

Carter G. Woodson, *The Miseducation of the Negro* (1933)

Zora Neale Hurston

Langston Hughes

Ralph Ellison, *The Invisible Man* (1952)

Gwendolyn Brooks, *A Street in Bronzeville* (1945)

James Baldwin, *The Fire Next Time* (1963)

Maya Angelou

Lorraine Hansberry, *To Be Young, Gifted, and Black* (posthumously published in 1969)

Nikki Giovanni

Tupac Shakur, *The Rose that Grew from Concrete* (posthumously published in 2000)

Art

Augusta Savage

Beauford Delaney

Loïs Mailou Jones

Romare Bearden

Gordon Parks

Gwendolyn Knight

Eldzier Cortor

Elizabeth Catlett

Jacob Lawrence

Faith Ringgold

Lorna Simpson

Jean-Michel Basquiat

Kara Walker

Music

James Weldon Johnson and John Rosamond Johnson, *Lift Every Voice and Sing* (1905)

Bessie Smith

Louis Armstrong

Mahalia Jackson

Sister Rosetta Tharpe

Billie Holiday

John Coltrane, *A Love Supreme* (1965)

Sam Cooke

Nina Simone

James Brown

Marvin Gaye, *What's Going On* (1971)

Aretha Franklin

Sly and the Family Stone, *There's a Riot Going On* (1971)

Roberta Flack & Donny Hathaway, *Roberta Flack & Donny Hathaway* (1972)

Stevie Wonder

The Isley Brothers, *Harvest for the World* (1976)

Erykah Badu, *Baduizm* (1997)

Lauryn Hill, *The Miseducation of Lauryn Hill* (1998)

Esperanza Spalding

Kendrick Lamar, *To Pimp a Butterfly* (2015)

Solange Knowles, *A Seat at the Table* (2016)

Film

Eyes on the Prize (1987), Produced by Henry Hampton

When We Were Kings (1996), Directed by Leon Gast

Selma (2014), Directed by Ava DuVernay

About the Author

Josiah Golson is an artist, lawyer, and writer from Chattanooga, Tennessee. He is the founder of the 800 Collective, a diverse group of artists using art as a means of civic engagement and public discourse. Josiah's work comprises of creative workshops, public art projects, and community development.

Born Randy Josiah Golson, Jr. in Tuscaloosa, Alabama in 1986, Josiah has been drawing since childhood. After earning a B.A. in Communication at the University of Tennessee at Chattanooga, Josiah attended the University of Texas School of Law, passing the Texas State Bar in 2013.

Made in the USA
Monee, IL
10 June 2020